KATABASIS:
A JOURNAL OF HEKATEAN DEVOTION & SCHOLARSHIP
VOL. 1, WINTER SOLSTICE 2021

PUBLISHER: SAM WEBSTER

EDITOR IN CHIEF: FAWN HEXE

COPY EDITORS: LUCERA A.F. & SCOTT WHITFIELD

ARTIST IN RESIDENCE: BOBBIE JAMES

CONTRIBUTING ARTISTS & AUTHORS:
JACK GRAYLE
HARPER FEIST
TAMARA WYNDHAM
DAVE PETERSON
DANIEL BRAN GRIFFITH

Copyright 2021 Fawn Russell
all contributed works are copyright their creators

All rights reserved. Except for brief quotations in a review, the book, or parts thereof, including the cover art and interior illustrations, must not be reproduced in any work without permission in writing from the publisher. The moral rights of the author have been asserted. For information contact: ConcrescentLLC@gmail.com
ISBN: 978-0-9903927-9-8
ISSN: 2770-9477

Concrescent Press
Richmond, California

"PROPLYAIA"
ARTIST IS BOBBIE JAMES

"PROPYLAIA" BY BOBBY JAMES
IV

"THE BODY OF HEKATE" BY FAWN HEXE
2

"HYMN TO HEKUBA" BY JACK GRAYLE
4

"BIRTH OF A STAR" BY TAMARA WYNDHAM
8

"HEKATE COMES" BY DANIEL BRAN GRIFFITH
9

DEVOTIONAL PROSE BY HARPER FEIST
10

"AT HER FEET" BY FAWN HEXE
15

"MEDUSA INVOCATION" BY DAVE PETERSON
16

"HEKATE TREE" BY FAWN HEXE
19

LIMINAL REVIEW: "LIBER KHTHONIA" BOOK
20

CONTRIBUTORS' BIOGRAPHIES
22

An Editorial: Body of Hekate

By Lamm Hexe

Hekate has so many epithets and faces. She is the dark sister in a long line of Goddesses: Kali, Lilitu, The Morrighan, Cerridwen, Ereshkigal, Hel. Hekate is a Titaness, a child of the Primordial Elders-those who were at the beginning and shall be at the end. She is the traveler between worlds, given dominion of Sea, Sky and Land by Zeus Himself. Her torches shine in the darkest corners of our psyche. She is a revealer of magick, patroness of Witchcraft, and cunning woman of poisonous herbs.

There are many speculations regarding Her origins, Her worship, Her place in the modern world of Paganry. Hekate is found in the highest of heavens and the deepest parts of earth. How can we work with this immense entity, especially since we are such small and insignificant beings? Do our prayers and shouts even matter to one who is eternal? Hekate has seen all and been known to help those whom She favors. How do we get on Her favorable side? Certainly no one would want to be on Her proverbial "shit list". As the one who aids in revenge, justice and the balancing of fairness, Hekate is swift in action and often without mercy. Her devotion is not one to be taken lightly.

I have never actually seen Hekate's true face. I have smelled and sensed Her like a garden. She is subtle, until She is not. She has made Her likes/dislikes known in small ways to me, but would only give hints or whispers before making the lesson learned. Hekate is aloof, yet familiar in our long term henontheist relationship. So I asked Her, "Why? Why have all my other spiritual experiences been very intense and swift, while You are slow, quiet, and hidden?" I wondered if perhaps I was not ready for Her to reveal Herself fully, or not accepting of Her communion...then She appeared.

It was accompanied at first with fear; afraid of what I might actually see in Her presence. All the hairs on my body stood up, the air became very still and out of my red devotional Brimo candle Her face formed, quickly. It kept changing though: a white face that looked like a screaming skull, then a full-faced woman in dancing flames, and finally into the peaceful repose of meditation. It changed a few times, each time clearer than the next. The fear subsided a little, becoming fainter in strength but still very much there. After Her revelation, I thanked Hekate and swore never to doubt Her presence in my life again. She can remain the Lady of Mysteries... I will keep my faith burning.

Devotional

Hymn to Hekuba

A rite to transform oneself into a Hound of Hekate
By Jack Grayle

Hekuba was the legendary queen who ruled Troy during the Trojan war. The regal wife of King Priam and mother of the warriors Hector and Paris and the prophetess Cassandra, she was fated to witness the ruthless destruction of her kingdom and family at the hands of the Greeks. One version of her myth tells that her grief and madness were such that, as she was being handed over to as a war-trophy to Odysseus, she snarled at him so fiercely that Hekate in her compassion transformed Hekuba into a black dog, thus allowing her to escape the ultimate humiliation of slavery.

It is the goal of every devotee of Hekate to become the Queen's faithful Hound, so this story has great value as a meditation both on Hekate's compassion and on the Devotee's ability to unbecome: to forsake her compromised self and take on new forms by which she may attain her freedom.

What follows is a Hymn to the ruined Queen of Troy, whereby the Devotee requests Hekuba to help her become a Hound of Hekate.

On the night of the new moon, in wild place, spin your strophalos and repeatedly call forth Hekate by the epithets PHILOSKYLAX, ATALOS and SKYLAKITIS. If she is slow to come, use the compulsion MASKELLI MASKELLO PHNOUNKENTABAOTH REXICHTHON HIPPOCHTHON PYREPEGANYX.

Then, when your hair rises on end and your flesh prickles at her approach, welcome her, and ask her to bear the following hymn to Queen Hekuba, who serves as her faithful Hound.

Begin the rite proper by drawing upon the ground Hekuba's name in ancient Greek, as set forth below:

Ἑκάβη

Pour out in a circle around the name an good-quality bottle of wine to honor Queen Hekuba's regal nature. Then, pour nephalia (honey water) onto the earth to honor her chthonic status. Finally, sprinkle dust taken from the grave of a mother who died young. Then, kneel and press your left hand to the wet earth, and call out the following Hymn:

Khaire, Khaire, Khaire, Hekuba!
Black servant in the black service of a black queen!
O royal hound! O curse unbound!
O cunning cur who knows the narrow nightroad's every bend,
And scours Styx's shore for fatal wraiths
Who crave the satisfaction of their end.
O hungerer who hunts the souls that serve
As Hekate's great quarry! Howler, prowler –
You harry hungry ghosts, and worry
The ranks of the restless dead.

Hail, Bitch! Hail, Queen! Hail, Hekuba!
You who fled the toppling towers of Troy
In another life. Wife of Priam
In another life. Mother of Hektor
In another life. Sorrower, sorrower,
Whose sorrowing mind combined
With so furious a soul that neither
Could be contained or defined
By the body they controlled,
And so departed.
O black, four-legged queen, hear my cry!
For I honor you and yours. But know:
I too have seen my kingdom burn;
I too loved those who did not return
From the field of battle; I too was handed over
To those who worked my ruin; I too
Suffered the flame, the chain, the lash, and my undoing.

Hekuba! Hear Me! And lend me, Queen
The gift of your good favor, for –

I too would slip my enemies, and become
A hunter, haunter, harrier –
I too would shed my skin to sink
Uncaught, unsought, unseen!
I too would track the restless ones
In the service of a black queen
As a black dog.
See this hand? I trade it for a black paw.
See this mouth? I trade it for a black maw.
See this head, this haunch, this heart?
Devour them all. Pull them apart. And in their place,
Give me the head, haunch, heart
Of an unbound hound; of a cunning cur. I am me
But as you were; and as you are, so I'll be.

(Press your brow to the earth and say:)

Hunter: I would be unbound: devour me.
Hunter: I would be unbound: devour me.
Hunter: I would be unbound: devour me.

HEKUBA RITE

Whereby a black dog may be summoned to guard and guide the Devotee in the form of her shadow.

On the night of the waxing moon, take rainwater and mud from a dog's pawprint, and mix it with alcoholic mead. In another container, add the bloody runoff of raw meat. Then, in the same solitary place that you performed the Hymn to Hekuba, call upon Hekate by her epithets as before. Then take a string soaked in accelerant and lay it in a circle. Kneeling within the circle, take the jaw of a dog and cut a furrow in the earth, into which a dog tooth will be laid. Once the tooth is buried in the furrow, pour the mix of rain and spirits on it, and then light the encircled string on fire. As you do so, say the following:

I till the earth with a dog's-jaw-plow
    In the name of Hekuba!

(Cut furrow)
I seed the earth with teeth now
    In the name of Hekuba!

(Press tooth into furrow and cover with earth)
I water the earth with rain from a paw
    In the name of Hekuba!

(Pour out rainwater onto the covered tooth)
I warm the earth with flame that I draw
From the heart of Hekuba!
(Ignite string so that a ring of fire appears about you.)
Still kneeling, put your hand over the buried tooth, and say the following:)

O Spirits of the Earth!
O Nyx, Styx, Khaos, Erebos,
Gaia, and all your sons and daughters:
Let this seed swell to shadow
Let shadow swell to fog
Let fog become flesh,
Let flesh become dog.

(Pour out the bloody runoff from fresh meat upon the earth where the tooth is buried, saying:)

Blood do I pour
So that the spell is pure
And finds favor with you,
O Gaia, O Nyx, Styx, Khaos, Erebos;
O spirits in and of the earth.

(Take a pinch of the mud that lies above the tooth and swipe it above and below your left eyelid, saying:)
May the spirit of that four-footed queen
Appear now in a form that may be seen
To guard and guide me ever after,
And lead me to the place I seek.

(Repeat the following conjuration again and again:)
KYNA * KYNA * BASILEIA
HEKUBA * HEKATE

(As you chant the words, hold your hand out so that the waxing moon throws your hand's shadow onto the earth where the tooth is buried. When you feel Hekuba's approach, move your fingers so that the shadow they cast is in the shape of the head of a dog. If the moon is obscured by cloud, use candle-light to throw the shadow. That shadow is Hekuba's epiphany; when it is cast, the Dog-Queen is present. Welcome her respectfully in your own words, and tell her that it is your will, as a Hierophant of Hekate, that she remain within your shadow henceforth, and as an extension of your shadow, that she aid, advise and protect you, in the ineffable name of Hekate.)
Adjure her by this final formula:

So shall you, Hound, reside within my shadow
And there aid and advise me in all ways,
For I adjure you
By the love you bore to Priam;
By the love you bore to Hektor;
By the love you bore to Paris;
By the love you bore to Cassandra;
By the love you bore to Troy,
And by the love you bore yourself, the great Queen of Troy;
And by your fury toward the Greeks,
And by your hatred of Helen,
And by your contempt for Achilles,
And by your loyalty to HEKATE SKYLAKITIS;
By these I bind you to me, by these unspeakable names:

MASKELLI * MASKELLO
PHNOUNKENTEBAOTH *
OREOBAZAGRA * REXICHTHON
HIPPOCHTHON * PYREPEGANYX

This ends the rite. Use her well, and with great respect. One day you will meet her face-to-face.

"This image of Hekate as the triple goddess was made by making contact body prints. I put paint on the model's body, and press it onto a surface. Then I paint color around it and in layers over it, working further with brushes, my fingers, airbrush, and splattered painting techniques. The layers, adding both physical and metaphorical substance, enhance the original print, as well as building up a glow, so that the aura becomes luminous. Later, I manipulated these imaged in the computer and added her name in ancient Greek, and the symbol used for the asteroid Hekate."

"BIRTH OF A STAR"
ARTIST IS TAMARA WYNDHAM

"HECATE COMES"
ARTIST IS DANIEL BRAN GRIFFITH

Devotional Prose Series

Words & Image
By Harper Feist

Baptized

Cancer, the woman said, and then hung up the phone
the airlock closed
the known universe behind
and unknown reality of pain and loss ahead
into a vast reach of vacuum and darkness
flayed, raw, naked, longing

I came to Her rites unknowing
unwilling
frightened, exhausted, lonely, sick
every remaining notion of the world as a kindly place
that gods are a force
interested in caring for mortals
gone...

The tumor in a glass jar of formalin
illuminated by a torch of animal fat
guttering in the examination room
She is there, but
I am marred, dismembered, flat, ugly, childish
then the mind-bending drugs
finally, the silence of ritual

I made her acquaintance in the most prosaic of places
setting the eggs and olive oil, lentils and water
on a rock with a plaque to the city fathers
furtively, invisibly, weakly, confused even of their purpose

Was I asking to live? Was I asking to die?

Something called to me, and I went
Those offerings were only the beginning
little did I know what else I would be giving to Her.

Confirmed

In the fourth year, I walk to the stone in the dark before dawn and give quail eggs, olive oil, nephalia...

Eyes averted, I walked from the offering stone
into the dead trees
I hear the crows behind me accepting the offering
they scream and fight for the morsels
I am compelled to walk back by an hour later
they have left me a possum's face in appreciation

Suddenly the monthly offerings are no longer enough -
reaching deeper:

I meet you somewhere in the saltwater swamp near Ipswich, MA

the pole with the clattering masks dangling
In the blistering dark at the crossroads
stinging flies and the plastic symphony of cattails
The sodden smell of decay and fertility
Ribs of a wooden dingy protruding from the mud
the skeleton of a broken animal
and the clatter of the masks in the wind, hollow
The animal fat torch sputtering in the wind

My hands reach out and draw the blackest mask to my face
it won't come off

Shriven

A thousand miles from home
lightning cleaves the sky
flashing red on the inside of my eyelids
I open the window to smell the petrichor
The black air falls inside
a slap and a caress
I am delirious with lack of sleep
days of fasting and prayer
Myrrh oil and cinnamon coat nearly everything
Come, come, come to me

Se kaleo, Mene, kaleo se

I indulge in a few moments of sleep
and then walk, stumbling, while pleading for a sign
Owl pellets, nine
A beautifully abused house key
in the river bottom
I sink to the ground
consumed with gratitude

Hallowed by handfuls of fur and bone
I lay the key on the dirty velvet
of my makeshift altar
Anointing everything, weeping
myrrh already saturating cloth, bones, skin
from days of attention

I prick my finger and feed the key
the serpent skin,
one of the new bones
then spittle on all the same surfaces

It is no longer ineffable:

I feel Her reaching to me
as I am seeking Her
A coldness intrudes in my bowels
every hair is lifted
I feel a sudden rush of power
a sexual tremor
shaking with lust
Abject hunger

I must leave the house
I run back to the river bottom
where more bones await my starving hands

Ordained

I don the emblems of my office
and swallow the plant
driving me inward
Inside is Her
My dark Mistress
teasing me again about not living in my body
"Taste your food"
is her current advice

But she is leading me somewhere
a place I defined and requested
It seems like a pillar
it's a massive leg
attached to a massive body
smelling of musk
and sexual fluids
Warm because of the sun
standing on sand
me, a tiny fragile thing

next to a behemoth

Before long, it is moving
unimaginably fast
wings? I can't tell
She is behind me and to the left
As I ask my questions
forged in ritual
annealed with research
sharpened with repetition
polished with poetry
The beast is sarcastic,
cruel even, but he offers me knowledge
and power
I was shown the edge of a precipice with a cliff
he has chosen me and one other
and he has a purpose in mind
When it is over
She leads me out
Her hound
I am stronger than ever, sensually
and enormously occupying space
The taxi driver is afraid of me
He can't even speak
I arrive home, fall into the sleep of death

And in the morning,
everything is different

Wedlock

I am in the forest
Infernal blade swathed with dried blood
and soot hanging from my belt
The offerings are the same
quail eggs, olive oil, lentils, nephalia
and milk and wine come too
No more offerings at the rock
These are deeper into the black woods
behind the lake
a three-way crossroads game trail

Epikaloumai se, Ekate
Aimopotis
Sarkophagos

I sing my invitation as
I lay out the defensive circle
place the offerings
the white ring in the green is beautiful
I breathe in the dusty air
and throw the knife into the center
of my milky circle
Blood erupts from the earth
the sod peels away
to reveal muscle
a thin layer of fat
and blood
So much blood

Her splashing
Me splashing
pouring, surging
I am Hers
She is mine
and when the doctor at the ER asks me
sarcastically
what the name of the blade is
I know the answer
It is a solemn oath
Sworn in gore and soil

It is me, serene and magnificent
and Her,
my Mistress.

In Gratitude

The words and advice of many teachers and fellow practitioners went into the development of ever-deepening practice. Some of them are well-known in our small community, most are not. The readers will recognize some pieces of ritual from books/practices that have been especially beneficial to me. Certainly, these people will recognize themselves.

My helper spirits, living and not, I thank you. You have inspired this work and in doing so, helped make me what I am today.

And to Her: I fear you; I love you. I long to know you; I long for you to know me.

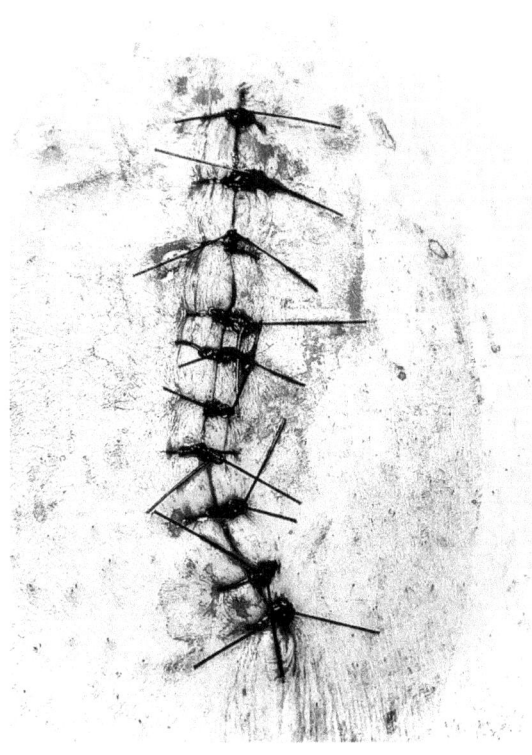

"Also she bore Asteria of happy name, whom Perses onceled to his great house to be called his dear wife. And she conceived and bare Hecate whom Zeus the son of Cronos honoured above all. He gave her splendid gifts, to have a share of the earth and the unfruitful sea. She received honour also in starry heaven, and is honoured exceedingly by the deathless gods. For to this day, whenever any one of men on earth offers rich sacrifices and prays for favour according to custom, he calls upon Hecate. Great honour comes full easily to him whose prayers the goddess receives favourably, and she bestows wealth upon him; for the power surely is with her. For as many as were born of Earth and Ocean amongst all these she has her due portion. The son of Cronos did her no wrong nor took anything away of all that was her portion among the former Titan gods: but she holds, as the division was at the first from the beginning, privilege both in earth, and in heaven, and in sea. Also, because she is an only child, the goddess receives not less honour, but much more still, for Zeus honours her."

- Hesiod, from "Theogony"

At Her Feet

Words & Image by Fawn Hexe

Sitting in silence, waiting to heed the call of mastery, the vision becomes clearer. What I thought was a deity is much more than that. She is a walker on the great axis of our Universe. Hekate is a psychopompos, a guide for the Dead. Her name means 'worker from afar', which makes sense as Hekate is not a very intimate presence... She is too busy to sit and hold our hands. She has the ability to travel throughout all dimensions, something most Gods cannot do. In Her earliest beginnings, it is believed Hekate was an imported Mother Goddess from Thessaly, Thrace or Persia, from the root 'Perses' alluded to by Herodotus (pg. 25, Rankine).

As a child of Titans, She played an unusual part in the battle against the Gods: assisting in the overthrow of Cronos by His children, the Olympians. For Her help, and maybe even due to fear as well, She was given access to all spheres of the universe by Zeus.

The roads traveled by Hekate are dark with only Her guiding torches and brazen sandals to light the way. It is at Her feet we can see where She begins. The bottoms of Her sandals are well-worn, having walked the length of the Universe again and back, guiding souls and sentient beings at Her choosing. Her toes sink into the Earth as roots, seeking out the darkest of places for nourishing stability. To worship and behold the sandal, to even be in the presence of Her eternal footwear, is something a true devotee would be in awe over should they ever meet this indomitable force. But oh, the places She can take us with those omnipresent feet!

At the beginning of any journey is the precipice...the starting line, the first steps we brave out onto the path. As Her devotees, we approach Hekate Propylaia ('one before the gate'), She who stands firmly with Her feet shining. Ancient devotees held shrines at the entrance to their dwellings, so should we hold sacred the hekataion: guardian and protector of the threshold. Here we may place obsidian on either side of the front entryway, reflecting all ill will from the home. We may hang a horseshoe above the doorway, upright to catch blessings. Here we leave behind the worries of our day, to gather in the twilight of Her presence. Here we wash Her feet and welcome Hekate into our home.

A Medusa Invocation Using the PGM

Words & Image
By David Peterson

> YOU ON EARTH HAVE UNWITTINGLY FELT ITS DISTANT PRESENCE—YOU WHO WITHOUT KNOWING IDLY GAVE TO ITS BLINKING BEACON THE NAME OF ALGOL, THE DAEMON-STAR. – H. P. LOVECRAFT

In Greek mythology, the Gorgon Medusa has the power to turn the living to stone with her gaze. After she is vanquished her head becomes a weapon on the shield of Athena or Zeus that turns enemies to stone. Athena defeats the Gorgon in some versions of the story, which earns her the epithet Gorgophona or Gorgon-slayer.(2) In Apollonius of Rhodes' Argonautica (3rd century BCE), the hero Perseus kills and beheads her, then gives her head to Athena. Although the Greek Magical Papyri (PGM) of the 1st to 5th centuries of the current era (CE) contain no explicit reference to Medusa, the description of Hecate as "serpent haired" is a clear allusion to the Gorgon. (3) Both the PGM and stellar magic give good reasons to work with Medusa herself using elements of the papyri.

Ancient sculpture and gems carved with Medusa's head are thought to have been considered apotropaic. Little is known about the magic performed with talismanic jewelry and other items that feature her, but she is associated with Algol in Behenian fixed star magic. Algol (Beta Persei) is located at approximately 26° degrees Taurus on the ecliptic and is the best-known star in the Perseus constellation. Algol represents Medusa's head carried in Perseus's left hand. Perseus and Taurus overlap in the sky so that Algol also serves as one of Taurus's bullseyes. Algol is derived from R'as al Ghul, the head of the demon in Arabic. As her name implies, she has a reputation as a wicked and fearsome ally both for protection and malefica, to make those bearing her talismans intimidating, to grant them victory, to freeze threats, and to send harm back to the attacker. Around 1490 in Northern Italy, Perseus, Medusa, and Algol were depicted in Trump 13 of the Sola Busca Tarocchi (4). In the Books of Occult Philosophy (published in the 1530s), using procedures derived from Arabic magic, Agrippa describes how to create talismanic rings by invoking Algol and other stars when they are in appropriate conjunction with the Moon.(5)

To my knowledge, no ancient invocations of Medusa are currently known but the PGM has tantalizing hints of the Medusa-Algol stellar tradition as much as 1000 years earlier than Agrippa and that major work of Arabic astrological magic, the Picatrix (11th century). As noted above, the Perseus constellation shows the hero standing with Medusa's head in his left hand. Graham describes several drawings in PGM XXXVI inspired by the constellation, which show gruesome figures holding a severed head in the left hand. (6)

Equally intriguing is the possible connection between Medusa and Akephalos or the Graeco-Egyptian headless god. The Headless Rite invokes a primordial god that controls all other spirits. The earliest known example of the rite is the Stele of Jeu the hieroglyphist in PGM V. 96-172. This was translated into English in 1852 and used for the Preliminary Invocation in the Goetia by Crowley and Mathers. (7) Later, Crowley used it as the basis for Liber Samekh, the Bornless Ritual, for magicians seeking to contact their magical assistant or Holy Guardian Angel. (8) Arguably, the Akephalos in the Stele of Jeu represents none other than Medusa. One of the voces magicae or barbarous names associated with Akephalos in the Stele of Jeu is AROGOGOROBRAO, which contains a corruption of GORGO, or Gorgon ("I call upon you, awesome and invisible god with an empty spirit, AROGOGOROBRAO SOCHOU MODORIO PHALARCHAO OOO"). Other candidates for Akephalos proposed by Graham are Osiris, Bes, and a demon in the Testament of Solomon. This does not mean there was a 1:1 association between Medusa and Akephalos; it seems likely that Akephalos encompasses aspects of Medusa, Osiris, Bes, and probably other deities and daimons as well. As with the transfer of attributes of Medusa to Hecate and Selene in PGM IV. 2785-2890, images of figures carrying heads and the barbarous names in Stele of Jeu and elsewhere make the papyri an excellent source for constructing a new-old invocation.

I wrote the following by cutting up and re-assembling portions of the PGM along with my own words. In her earliest iconography Medusa appears monstrous, while by Roman times, beautiful images of her are common. The first half invokes Medusa's more terrifying form, while the second appeals to her beauty and sympathy in asking for her aid. The invocation is designed to anchor the power of Algol to an appropriate talisman during a lunar conjunction on the ascendant or at midheaven. According to Agrippa, the herbs to use in invoking Algol are Mugwort and Hellebore (Hellebore is toxic, do not ingest it and use only Mugwort for incense), and the stone is Diamond. The following is brief and intended to be repeated in the time leading up to a conjunction while the talisman is suffumigated in the incense.

Hail Algol, Medusa!
Child of Echidna and Typhon
Daughter of Chaos
Tormentor, Justice, Destroyer,
Dark with serpent's scales
And the hair of serpents
Serpent-girded, who drink blood
And freeze all with your gaze
Nether, nocturnal, and frightful one
Before whom daimons quake in fear
And gods and heroes tremble

O beautiful Medusa,
I burn for you this incense
Be gracious and kind, you
Who exalt your children
Protect me, your child
From this day forward
Ensoul this talisman,
Make me victorious,
And return all harm
To whence it came

Endnote: Algol is known as the most protective star in the sky but can also cause mischief, including the disruption of electronics. She is made of a triplicity of stars, one brighter than the others, and has frequent eclipses when she "blinks out." It is advised to avoid working with her during those times. She can also take an initiatory role by stirring up uncomfortable situations that teach one to stay cool in adversity, a useful skill to learn and hone.

(<?>) H. P. Lovecraft, "Beyond the Wall of Sleep," in Beyond the Wall of Sleep, Arkham House, 1943.

(2) PGM XVIIIb. 1-7 in Hans Dieter Betz, ed., The Greek Magical Papyri in Translation, University of Chicago Press, 1996.

(3) Hecate is described as serpent haired and serpent girded in adjoining lines of PGM IV (2863-2864).

4) Peter Mark Adams, The Game of Saturn, Scarlet Imprint, 2017.

(5) Heinrich Cornelius Agrippa, Writings of Heinrich Cornelius Agrippa (1486-1535), digital editions by Joseph H. Peterson accessed 28/16/2021 at http://www.eso-tericarchives.com/agrippa/index.html. Also see the discussion of Agrippa in Christopher Warnock, Fixed Star, Sign & Constellation Magic, Renaissance Astrology, 2019.

(6)Lloyd D. Graham, "Perseus, Mars and the figurae magicae of PGM XXXVI," accessed 30/06/2021 at https://www.academia.edu/28232099/Perseus_Mars_and_the_figu-rae_magicae_of_PGM_XXXVI.

(7) Aleister Crowley, ed., and S. L. MacGregor Mathers, The Book of the Goetia of Solomon the King, Society for the Propagation of Religious Truth, 1904.

(8) Aleister Crowley, Magick: Book 4 parts I-IV, Samuel Weiser, 1994.

"HEKATE TREE"
ARTIST IS FAWN HEXE

Liminal Review

"Liber Khthonia" book review

By Fawn Hexe

> "We are Witches. We are by force masters of will, and when we realize our potential, we have the power to manifest our desires. We make mountains tremble, stir the sea to rage or calm it, we break the jaws of serpents without words and spells, and bid the dead to rise from their tombs"—
>
> Cullen, p. 1

The opening to Jeff Cullen's work "Liber Khthonia" is exactly what I expected from this long-time devotee of Hekate's cult. And yes, it is a cult by very definition. A "new religious movement" to be specific...because as Cullen points out throughout his text very adequately, there is no unbroken tradition to follow. He also shares this sentiment in his very modern approach to witchcraft, an often misunderstood magickal tradition without a tradition so to speak. Which is what inspires Cullen's premise for writing this book: helping others to develop a private cult praxis with Hekate. With some universality, anyone can adapt this technology for personal spiritual growth as a devotee or in a working magickal relationship with Her.

First, the nitty gritty: I loved the design of this book. Kudos to Allan Spiers for his beautiful aesthetic touch, one we fans often in the works of this power couple. So many fine art books are printed with gold gilded pages...but this came in silver; so appropriate to the lunar qualities of Hekate. The typeface was beautifully elegant, with the layout perfectly giving plenty of white space. The very clever thing I geeked out on: the footnotes were paragraphed in the outer margins right NEXT to the accompanying text! No looking in the back of the book or even at the bottom of the page. This was a book designed with the reader in mind...and it shows. The artwork is incredibly beautiful and original, as to be expected of Cullen. His depictions of deities and spirits, his working relationship with them all and his contributions to the Hekatean community have become legendary. We all knew he would write this book one day, and are glad he finally did.

Cullen has taken his years of devotion and magick with Hekate to a level deeply informed by ancient texts, but rooted in modern practice. "Liber Khthonia" is more than a grimoire, as the author included fun personal anecdotes, shedding light on a background preparing for the work he had ahead. I loved how Cullen tackled the subject of Hekate's historical roots and references.

Looking at Homer, Ovid, and Orpheus as sources always excites me with Hekate. He handled with grace the often taboo and uncomfortable issue of many modern Hekatean books: the "Maiden Mother Crone" problem. Really, he gives credit to the recent work of Sorita d'Este in her "Circle of Hekate: Vol. 1" - the first mention of Hekate as Crone being postmodern Aleister Crowley.

What I found to be especially groundbreaking was his approach to writing about curse work, a refreshing topic to see in modern Hekate materials. Cullen's exploration of ethics and witchcraft towards the end of this grimoire is very much aligned with my own experiences...both with Hekate and as a whole:

"Witches for thousands of years remained feared because of their immunity to conventional ethics and morality. We have a reputation for being judge, jury and executioner. We must ask ourselves how we will handle this responsibility. Will we be corrupt, maniacally cursing anyone who offends us, or will we be just, only employing our dark arts on those who truly deserve the effort based on our subjective opinion? Every curse a witch performs is another drop on the stone, slowly eroding it, every blessing is the sun that dries the drop before it hits the stone." (p.263)

Another thing I am totally taking away from this book is all the interesting ways Cullen suggests to use Hekate's tools. In particular, I was intrigued by his employment of cauldrons. Working with planetary metals and appropriate materials in conjunction with Hekate over the past several years I continue to travel through the spheres... so this connexion spoke to me. Cullen's insight into the device was what I needed for my own praxis, especially the "The Cauldron of Tartaros", something akin to a spiritual oubliette. Filled with dirts that have never seen the sun, a vessel for cursing and storing things which should not be seen nor touched...what witch wouldn't want one?

Speaking of curses, Cullen provides many juicy tidbits to integrate with any practice of witchcraft. Instructions for creating potions and powders as "Gorgon's Venom", "Destruction Oil", and "Black Unguent", a particularly nasty paste to spread on poppets, candles and other malefic tools....but so toxic and scary it requires gloves. Many of the ingredients Cullen includes are somewhat similar in their applications, if one were so inclined to really get into his concoctions acquiring some staple goods would be beneficial; i.e. snakeskin, black pepper, graveyard dirt, sulphur, many baneful herbs including henbane and datura, human ashes/powdered remains, black iron oxide, etc.

Cullen's craft is practical, highly concentrated in its effectiveness, and creatively informed by many different paths of magic. He has also assured me there are still copies available of this grimoire. I very much suggest any serious Hekatean collector and/or witch to snatch up a copy before they are all gone.

Liber Khthonia: A Contemporary Witchcraft and Devotional Tradition of Hekate by Jeff Cullen.
Published in Chicago, IL. by Brujo Bros, LLC. Artist's Edition, 2020. 328 pages.

Biographies

Tamara Wyndham

Tamara Wyndham has been making art all her life; encouraged by her mother, an artist. Born and raised in Los Angeles, California, she studied traditional drawing and painting at California State University, Long Beach; and more experimental drawing, book works, and performance at the University of California at Irvine.

Ms. Wyndham has been awarded artist residencies at the Henry Street Settlement, the Kate Millett Art Colony, the Vermont Studio Center, the Mariz Ceramic Workshop in the Czech Republic, Fundación Valparaíso in Mojácar, Spain, and an artist's fellowship from Earthwatch to work in Orce, Spain.

David Peterson

David Peterson has practiced magic in various ways since he was a teenager. He has a Ph.D. in Anthropology and after years of truancy, proved that if you put your mind to it you can do anything, and became a professor so he could teach other people's kids his bad habits. He is also an archaeologist, a spectroscopist, and specializes in prehistoric archaeology of the Russian steppes and Caucasus. He is writing a book about metallurgy and shamanism in the Middle Volga region during the Bronze Age and currently resides in St. Paul, Minnesota.

Harper Feist

Harper Feist has been immersed in various magically related endeavors since she was a teenager. She is currently involved in formal Thelemic organizations (O.T.O. and A∴A∴) and teaches a class on scrying at the Blackthorne School. In her mundane life, she's a Ph.D. scientist and a martial artist. Her love of poetry bridges all these interests.

Jack Grayle

Jack Grayle is a longtime devotee of Hekate. He has led workshops and rituals throughout the US, and has taught at the Woolston-Steen Theological Seminary. His book, The Hekataeon, is a 368-page grimoire filled the hymns, songs, spells, chants, invocation, incantations, and a complete self-initiation in the mysteries of the eternal and ineffable Hekate.and meaning of folklore, legend and Sacred Mythology. Daniel describes himself as an Esoteric Folklorist but has himself, been called a little man with a big mind.

Biographies

Bobbie James

Hecate devoted witch and artist, Bobbie James has been creating work inspired by darker aspects of nature, femininity and the occult for over 15 years. Magical energy and emotional expression is seen through her use of paint, pastels, charcoal, and ink. Elements from rituals are mixed with an art medium and applied to many of her works. Often nudity is present in her art, vulnerability is the idea behind its use revealing or stripping away the hidden.

Daniel Bran Griffith

Daniel Bran Griffith is a Registered Nurse living in central England. Frequently writing under the pseudonym 'The Chattering Magpie,' he has seen his work published in more than a dozen Pagan, Folklore or Occult related anthologies, journals and magazines. Daniel is the founder and Robin of the Hearth of the Turning Wheel, an independent coterie based in old Mercia. His particular area of interest is the symbolism and meaning of folklore, legend and Sacred Mythology. Daniel describes himself as an Esoteric Folklorist but has himself, been called a little man with a big mind.

Submission Guidelines for Publication

Overview
A labour of love, a devotional work in the vein of academic scholarship and continued Bhakti relationship with the titaness Hekate defines this journal. This body of work is an inspirational tool committed to the furthering of research, sharing of experiences and honouring the influence of Hekate in our modern lives.

The Basics
This journal is for Hekate, first and foremost. Secondly, it is scholarly, poetic, expressive gifts in Her honor. With Her recent popularity, Hekate has become an inspiration the world over and many are moved to create in their passion for Her.
We ask that all text be submitted as attached Word documents or embedded in a singular email. All images should be in TIFF or JPG format as well. High resolution scans are recommended, no larger than 600 dpi. Our printing will be in greyscale, so be aware anything colorful or digitally photographed will be formatted to accommodate this ink choice. All text and artwork submitted must be original and have never been published elsewhere, including in both digital and physical formats.

Spelling
Canadian/UK/Australian spellings and American spellings are generally the English ways of writing.. If submissions are in a language other than English, the author must provide a translation and type.

Language Styles
Except for in the cases of poetry or art, we would prefer the text to remain in a modern English language format, avoiding such arcane grammar as "thine", "thy" or other old-fashioned ways of spelling.

Citations, Footnotes, and Bibliography
If not already formatted to this style, our editors here at Katabasis will make sure all footnotes and citations are uniform. We prefer the Chicago Manual of Style when making these notations. Please see example:

Crowley, Aleister Gems from the Equinox: Instructions by Aleister Crowley for His Own Magical Order, (Chicago: Weiser Books, 2007), pp. 26-31.

www.ingramcontent.com/pod-product-compliance
Lightning Source LLC
Chambersburg PA
CBHW071214100426
42735CB00047B/2852